Motorhomes
A first-time-buyer's guide

DISCARD

www.rac.co.uk
www.veloce.co.uk

This publication has been produced on behalf of RAC by Veloce Publishing Ltd. The views and the opinions expressed by the author are entirely his own, and do not necessarily reflect those of RAC.

First published in July 2012 by Veloce Publishing Limited, Veloce House, Parkway Farm Business Park, Middle Farm Way, Poundbury, Dorchester, Dorset, DT1 3AR, England. ISBN: 978-1-845844-49-3 UPC: 6-36847-04449-7

Fax 01305 250479/e-mail info@veloce.co.uk
web www.veloce.co.uk or www.velocebooks.com.

the driving people

Motorhomes
A first-time-buyer's guide

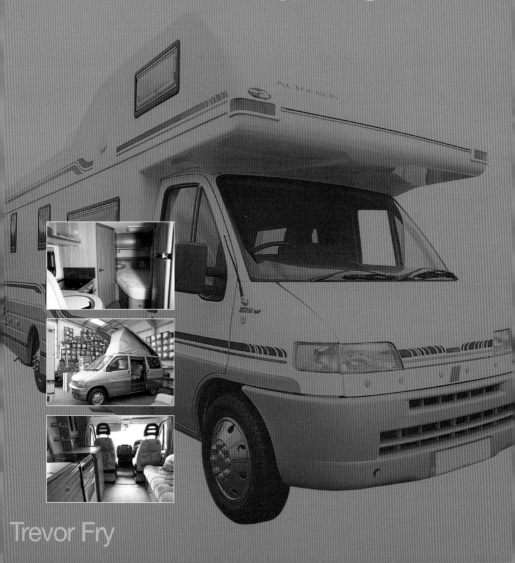

Trevor Fry

Contents

Introduction

Who the book is for

Packed with good advice from an experienced motorhomer, this book is for anyone contemplating the purchase of their first campervan or motorhome.

Why buy this book?

The book is written in plain English with full colour pictures throughout. It shows you many of the different types of campervan and motorhome that are on the market.

Coverage includes buying a new or secondhand unit from a dealer or, privately, from an individual.

A wealth of images give you an indication of what layouts room and storage facilities you can expect when comparing a basic van conversion to a much larger A-Class vehicle.

It shows you what you may expect as regards internal refinements, ie heating, hot water, etc, within either a new or used van. Also, any of the many extras you may consider fitting or having fitted to make the van your own.

Trevor Fry

Thanks to Tom Lower of Somerset Motorhome Centre for allowing the use of his vehicles.

one

Essentials

Firstly, it should be said that purchasing a motorhome involves a compromise between what you want and what's available. If you find your ideal motorhome style, with the engine and layout exactly as you want, then you're that one-in-a-million motorhomer!

This book is intended for both the first-time buyer, and those returning to motorhoming after a break. It discusses the types of motorhome available, and the most common layouts. It covers what to look for, what questions to ask, and what you can expect for your money.

Your biggest consideration should be comfort: you may be using it for a long time, and so, if you're uncomfortable, the joy of motorhoming may soon be lost. Try out everything, including the bed: that converted dinette may call itself a double, but is it really big enough? The walk in shower: walk in, yes, but can you turn around in it?

This book makes no distinction between campervans and motorhomes, although campervans are generally smaller and used for shorter trips.

Check your driving licence before you start looking, as this may dictate the size of the motorhome you can drive without having to take a further test.

The government, and, therefore, the police, use the Maximum Authorised Mass (MAM) as a guide. MAM is the total weight of a vehicle, plus anything it can safely carry. You'll need to make

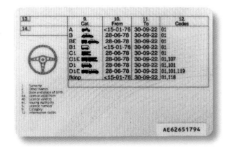

Fig 1. Rear of UK driving licence showing different classes of vehicle.

sure your driving licence has the correct vehicle category for you to drive larger motorhomes.

Category B
Covers vehicles with a MAM of up to 3500kg, with up to eight passenger seats, and with a trailer no heavier than 750kg.
It's also permissible to tow a trailer heavier than 750kg if the MAM of the vehicle and trailer combined is no more than 3500kg. A trailer must also be lighter than the vehicle that tows it. To tow a trailer heavier than 750kg you'll need a category B+E licence.

Fig 1a. Vehicle weight plate.

Category C1
Covers vehicles with a MAM greater than 3500kg, but less than 7500kg, with a trailer no heavier than 750kg. To tow a heavier trailer you'll need a category C1+E licence.

Category C
Covers vehicles with a MAM over 3500kg, and with a trailer no heavier than 750kg. To tow a trailer that weighs more than 750kg you will need category C+E.

This information was taken from: www.direct.gov.uk/en/Motoring/DriverLicensing/WhatCanYouDriveAndYourObligations/DG_10037875.

The site also contains details of the maximum size of motorhomes allowed on UK roads (if you're thinking of importing), and also how to import and register vehicles for the UK.

How do you intend to use your motorhome?
Everyday transport
Whilst some people use small, van-type motorhomes for everyday transport, this could prove rather costly. Increasingly, insurers are asking about expected annual mileage, or whether the vehicle will be used for commuting, and then adjusting premiums to suit. Size is a major consideration when using a motorhome for everyday use, not only when driving around town, but parking, too: not many shopping centres have parking areas that can take a 24ft motorhome. Also, motorhomes aren't as economical with fuel as a car, even less so when driving around town. Small, van-type pop-tops or high-tops could be everyday drivers, of course, and would certainly be more practical than a 28ft A-Class type.

Weekends away
If weekends away are on your agenda, then the first question should be how many berths are required? Do you want a small two-berth, or something for four people, or even more?
Is it a case of there generally being just the two of you, but occasionally the children/grandchildren might come along? Do you intend using it only in the summer, or all year round? These considerations make a big difference to the type of motorhome you might need. For example, two teenage children could sleep in an awning or safari room in the summer, so a two-berth panel van with seating for four might suffice.

If the children are small, however, then perhaps a 2+2-berth pop-top might be all that's needed for year-round motorhoming.

Once you've decided on the number of berths, and whether or not you'll be a year-round camper, what other equipment will you need? Onboard water tanks, maybe, if you intend staying on sites with hot and cold water not far away, or will you be wild camping (not on a site at all)? It may be nice to have a marine or cassette toilet, but would a porta-potti suffice? Do you really need a fitted shower in the motorhome if it's only for weekend use? Mains electricity is ideal, but do you need it? A good-sized leisure battery, 85 amp hours or greater, should be enough for the weekend. A single gas bottle would keep you going for a few trips, and refills are readily available.

Touring holidays, UK

Here we're looking at longer holidays in the motorhome, and again the question of the number of berths needs to be decided, as does whether the van will be used in the summertime only or year-round. If you're intending to spend quite a bit of time in your motorhome, a larger van may be necessary, and equipment not deemed essential for a weekend away could become so on a longer trip. If travelling further afield, bear in mind that sites may be few and far between, or you may have decided that wild camping is for you: if so, onboard water tanks, toilet, and shower unit may be necessities. Sites offering mains hook-up facilities mean you can charge your leisure batteries, or solar panels could keep them topped up when on the move. The ability to carry a spare gas bottle may be important if you intend to wild camp, but we'll cover more about extras in chapter six.

Touring holidays, abroad

Touring abroad generally means longer holidays, increased mileage, and more equipment essential for your comfort. Although some people can manage in a small, two-berth Volkswagen camper, others may want all the luxuries of home living. An awning or a safari room is a good idea in a hot country, where you could be spending a lot of time relaxing outside, enjoying the weather with a glass of wine (more about awnings and safari rooms later).

One important consideration to bear in mind is that calor gas isn't available in some countries, and an alternative is a bulk LPG tank. Bear in mind that different countries use different LPG hose adaptors, and some require that the inlet be on the exterior of the body rather than inside the gas cabinet (you may not be allowed to fill up in the case of the latter).

Living in your motorhome

Are you intending to live in your motorhome full-time? If so, how much room do you need (it's surprising just how many belongings you collect through a lifetime)?

What would happen if you or your partner are taken seriously ill, the motorhome is involved in an accident, or suffers a major breakdown? A cautionary tale in this respect is that of the motorhome that was involved in an accident in Spain, which was driven by the owner to the Hymer factory in Germany, from where he phoned his insurance company with reference to repairing it. He was told that the work could only be done in the UK, so had to return there to have the repair done (at twice the cost).

two

What type of motorhome?

New or used?
Not as big a question as you might think, and more to do with how much the vehicle will cost to buy and run.

A small, secondhand, two-berth van conversion can be had from about £2000 – or you could splash out on a brand new, six- to eight-berth RV for

Fig 2. New motorhome circa 2010.

Fig 3. Used motorhome circa 1994.

£150,000+. Bear in mind that bigger and newer motorhomes will have higher insurance premiums, though.

There's also the cost of servicing to consider, and where you may have to take it to get it done. Some insurers are beginning to insist that motorhomes are serviced by a VAT-registered garage, and that there is a yearly habitation check – all of which adds to your costs.

Where are you going to store it? Some properties have a covenant stating what can and cannot be kept on them, a consideration that could well influence your course of action.

Whether buying secondhand or new, be ready to barter over the price: dealers will be especially keen to make a sale to keep stock turning over. Buying new from a dealer will give you the benefit of a warranty, so if the dealer concerned is not prepared to come down on price, ask for an extension of the warranty, or for a few extras – such as a mains hookup cable or an extra leisure battery – to be included in the price. If, despite your best efforts, the dealer won't play ball, try asking him to remove his company sticker from the window of the vehicle so that at least you're not providing him with free advertising!

Do your research and go and look at lots of motorhomes. Talk to existing owners of various models: most will be more than happy to tell you about their experiences, which should give you an idea of what you're looking for. If buying secondhand, ask to see service history paperwork. It's all too easy for a seller to claim that "the cambelt's just been changed," but statements like that should be disregarded if there's no paperwork to back them up.

A secondhand motorhome from a dealer will generally cost more than if bought privately because the dealer has overheads. If the dealer has taken the motorhome in part exchange, he may well try to recoup some of the discount given when he sells it on. Most dealers will offer a warranty of some sort, normally 3-12 months, depending on the age of the motorhome, so paying £1500-£1800 more for a dealer sale as opposed to a private sale could make sense for a 12 month warranty, but probably not for only three months. You could just ask for a 12 month warranty; you never know, you might just get it!

When you find a motorhome that you like, ask to take it for a test drive – that's you driving, not the salesman! You need to know what it feels like behind the steering wheel; can you reverse it, for example, and are there any reversing sensors, or a reversing camera? Try to imagine what you might feel like after a two- or three-hundred mile drive: relaxed and comfortable or tense and aching?

Take your time looking over the vehicle, paying particular attention to the corners, as this is where motorhomes tend to get knocked and water starts to seep in. Look carefully at all the water-carrying pipes, but keep in mind that the seller may have drained the water, so you may not be able to tell if there are any leaks. If you can do so safely, get onto the roof and examine all the edge joints, the satellite mountings, and solar panel mounts, checking that they are secure. Look for mould or moss in all the outside joints: a sure sign of water laying there, or possible water ingress.

If the seller tries to get you to buy the motorhome there and then, remember that anything he offers will still be available tomorrow, or whenever

you go back. If you do decide it's the one for you, leave and go home, go for a coffee, or just take a walk to consider your decision *away* from the vehicle and the seller.

If you're buying secondhand, consider how easy it will be to get spare parts for the engine, body, and internal fittings.

Mileage
This is a tricky subject because, unlike a car that may have been used every day, a motorhome may only travel 5000 miles a year, so a ten-year-old model may have just 50,000 miles on the clock. If you're not knowledgeable in this area, I suggest you have the motorhome inspected by the RAC, as this will at least give you some indication of the condition of the engine. Also, if available, old MoT certificates will give an idea of what mileage has been covered over what period.

Power steering
Power steering is something we tend to take for granted these days, but it is a major consideration when buying a secondhand motorhome, which may not be apparent until you have been driving for a couple hundred miles. Motorhomes are heavy. Some sellers will say: "It hasn't got power steering, but is still easy to manoeuvre," but remember that they are trying to sell the motorhome. Out on your test run, try and imagine taking a 200-300 mile journey in the vehicle. Will driving feel comfortable, or will your arms be hanging off?

Left- or right-hand drive?
Left-hand drive motorhomes can be slightly cheaper, as they are mostly imported models. Hymer is a German manufacturer of A-Class and coachbuilt motorhomes. If you intend to do a lot

of driving abroad then left-hand drive could be considered an advantage. If you only wish to tour in the UK, perhaps you would feel better with a right-hand drive motorhome? The consensus of opinion amongst motorhomers is that it's easier to drive a left-hand drive vehicle in the UK than it is to drive a right-hand drive vehicle abroad. But, at the end of the day it's down to you and how you feel about this.

Whilst on the subject of an imported motorhome, if it's your intention to use it all year round, imported motorhomes, in general, are winterised to a higher standard (better insulation in the floors, walls, and roof, and inboard or underslung water tanks that are well insulated) than those produced in the UK, although it's fair to say that UK-built motorhomes are now starting to catch up.

Importing your motorhome
If the thought of acquiring a (probably) higher specification motorhome for a lower price appeals, you could consider this option. If you know someone who has already done this, ask him how he did it; firsthand knowledge is priceless.

Foreign dealers will likely know what paperwork is required to export a motorhome to the UK, and it's this side of things that you will probably require help with. How do you register the van for UK roads without UK plates? How do you get insurance for a foreign plated vehicle? Well, the DVLA will issue you with plates that are recorded against the chassis number, subject to the correct paperwork, and it will be the same with regard to third party insurance. One question you do need to answer is; does the vehicle need an MoT?

If you take your time, there's no reason why you can't import your own motorhome from a dealer. Whether buying abroad privately is as simple is

another matter: I would imagine that the seller could help you with the European side of things – provided you both speak the same language.

The Department of Transport offers lots of advice on how to import a vehicle, and also addresses the question of whether or not VAT is due on the import. This government website may be a good place to begin your research: http://www.vca.gov.uk/vca/other/faqs-vehicle-importi.asp

Fuel types
Diesel
Readily available in the UK and Europe, note that newer, lighter vans can return sensible mileage per gallon – 30-40mpg, if not more – depending on size and type.

Older vans that do not have a turbocharged engine can sometimes also return more sensible miles to the gallon – 30mpg, say – but this is at the cost of a slight loss of power, and compares with 25mpg for the same age motorhome with a turbocharged engine. Diesel is the most expensive fuel on the market at the moment.

Bio-fuels
Slowly coming onto the market, but yet to make any sort of inroad into the motorhome market.

Petrol
Readily available, petrol (gasoline) tends to be used mostly in the smaller panel vans, classic vans like the VW Bus, or for older coachbuilt motorhomes. Miles per gallon can be comparable with diesel vans, though some claim that a diesel engine will last longer, due to its simpler design and low rpm torque.

LPG
Not so readily available, but beginning to spread across the UK, this is

generally used in converted petrol (gasoline) engines, with the possibility of automatically changing fuel type from petrol to LPG, and vice versa, without stopping the engine. One thing to note is that if you intend touring aboard, you may need as many as six to eight different adaptors to make the various continental filling station nozzles fit into your LPG tank. At the time of writing, LPG is cheaper than either petrol or diesel.

Disability
Motorhomes can be purchased with automatic gearboxes, and a standard motorhome can be adapted so that the accelerator, brake, and clutch are operated by paddles fitted behind the steering wheel, rather than foot-operated pedals.

What size motorhome?
When considering the type of motorhome you want, whilst it may seem appealing to have a larger model, be aware that some sites do not allow the larger motorhomes such as fifth wheel, large A-Class, coachbuilt, and American-style RVs. The limit seems to be around 26-28ft. And even if the site you intend to use doesn't restrict size, you could find that access is impossible. Remember, too, that 24ft becomes 26ft with a bike rack or back box on the back, and 9ft high becomes over 11ft when a roof box or a satellite dish is added. So, be honest with yourself: driving a motorhome can be fun, but if the model you choose proves too large or too heavy, then the fun will be lost. There's no point going away for a weekend break if you need the whole weekend to recover from getting there ...

Now would be a good time to recheck your licence, so that you don't fall in love with a vehicle you wouldn't be permitted to drive.

When considering which type of motorhome you think you would like, pay particular attention to layout and the vehicle's payload.

Payload
This refers to the 'spare' weight left over after calculating the maximum technical permissible laden mass (MTPLM, also known as MAM), minus the mass in running order (MIRO). Sounds like double Dutch? Let me explain. MTPLM is the permissible weight of the vehicle when it is fully laden to maximum capacity, and MIRO is the minimum weight of the vehicle when empty, but with what could be considered the basics (fuel, water and driver) on board. Different manufacturers include or exclude varying items from their MIRO, however. If possible, it would be a good idea to get the van weighed carrying what *you* might consider to be the essentials, so that you are fully aware of its payload. Remember that every accessory you add to a motorhome will eat into your available payload – that extra gas bottle, the satellite dish, bikes, etc. So, whilst a 500kg payload may seem a lot, if there are four of you that allowance will soon disappear.

Some imported motorhomes have been down-plated to appeal to a wider audience: ie, a 4.2-ton motorhome plated for 3.5-ton, but of course this leads to a smaller payload than the chassis could safely carry. It's possible to have it re-plated, or even get your motorhome upgraded – which may prove a cheap option, and only involve a new plate – or it could prove extremely costly as it may involve not only uprating the suspension, but also new axles, brakes, etc.

Whilst on the subject of payloads, a lot of motorhomes have ladders and roof racks onto which you can fit a top box. Bear in mind, though, that there will be a weight limit with regard to what can be put on the roof – sometimes as little as 75kg.

Some vans will have a plate that will state not only the MTPLM, but also the maximum weight per axle, which can be handy if you have a tag axle van (one front axle and two rear axles). Knowing this value means you can take your motohome to a weighbridge and have each axle weight taken to show the weight distribution to confirm it's safely loaded.

In fact, for peace of mind I would recommend that you take the unloaded van to a weighbridge and record its weight. Then take it back after loading and have it weighed again: I believe you'll be rather surprised how much it weighs carrying only what you consider to be the essentials. A friend of mine did just this, and discovered his motorhome was 1.2 tons overweight!

The following example should give you an idea of what to consider. A 15 stone driver eats into your available payload by about 95kg. If your payload is 600kg, and there are four of you, you could find over half your payload weight has been acounted for before you've packed anything! Then there's the satellite system, the bikes on the rear rack, or even a motor scooter, the safari room ... Oh dear; no payload left!

Remember: if your motorhome is involved in an accident and is overweight, your insurance company won't be too pleased. Apart from anything else, the vehicle's brakes will not have been designed to stop anything over and above its designated maximum weight.

Towing with a motorhome

A vehicle's weight plate may contain a value for something called maximum train weight: the maximum weight of the motorhome, plus a trailer of specified maximum weight.

You'll often see motorhomes towing cars on something called an A-frame, but this is a grey area in the UK, legally speaking, in relation to the towing fittings, brakes, and lights relative to the towed vehicle. Some motorhome websites – despite having contacted the DVLA – still can't say categorically what is and isn't correct. Some drivers, concerned about this situation, opt to tow a small trailer with a car on it (although some automatic cars or 4x4s can't be towed using an A-frame). Whichever system you intend to use, check with your insurer that you are covered for it.

At the time of writing, it would appear that it is not allowed to tow a car on an A-frame in Italy, Spain or Germany, BUT – and it is a big but – it all depends on interpretation of EU law. A car on an A-frame cannot become a 'trailer' as it's not designed to be used like that, but one possible way around this is that, if your motorhome is registered in the UK (where A-frames are 'permitted'), under EU law, it is also permitted anywhere *within* the EU. I hasten to add, however, that I would not like to test this theory!

Carrying a motor scooter on a rack at the rear of the motorhome

If you intend to fit a rack and/or carry a motor scooter on the rear of your motorhome, take particular care to note the effect it will have on overall payload, and handling of your motorhome.

Use the following calculation to determine the effects of the extra weight:

Calculation 1
NEW front axle
load (NEW AF) = AF-(LDx(OH/WB))

Calculation 2
NEW rear axle
load (NEW AR) = AR+LD+(AF-NEW AF)

Where:
AF = the front axle load (as per the weight plate)
AR = the rear axle load (as per the weight plate)
WB = wheelbase (measured from the centre of the front axle to the centre of the rear axle)
OH = overhang (measured from the centre of the rear axle to the centre of the rack)
LD = weight of rack and motor scooter

Here's an example:
Our van has an AF of 1500kg and an AR of 2000kg, which is quite common for a 3500kg motorhome.

The LD – the motor scooter (complete with oils, fuel, etc) and rack weight – weighs 200kg.

The WB is 3000mm, and the OH is 1000mm.

Using the figures above:
NEW AF is 1500-(200 x (1000/3000)) =1433.33kg
NEW AR is 2000+200+ (1500/1433.33) = 2266.67kg

The effect is that the front axle weight is reduced by approximately 77kg, but the weight on the rear axle has increased by approximately 267kg. You'll now need to check these new gross figures against the plated figures to see if the vehicle is overloaded, or just check what your new payload would be.

One other thing to be aware of is that travelling over speed humps creates a bounce that can increase LD weight by anything up to 50 per cent, so proceed cautiously in such situations.

What type of layout?
The physical layout of the van is crucial to your comfort, and requires the same amount of consideration as deciding on the type of motorhome you want.

Bear in mind that the number of berths you require will have an influence on the type of layouts available to you.

Major considerations

Bed: fixed or not?
The benefits of a fixed bed layout are that the bed is always in place, can be left made up, and it has a large amount of storage underneath. In most cases,

Fig 4. Fixed bed (note cut-off corner [arrowed] to improve access to the toilet).

Above: Fig 5. Fixed bed.   Below: Fig 6. Fixed bed (bathroom across rear).

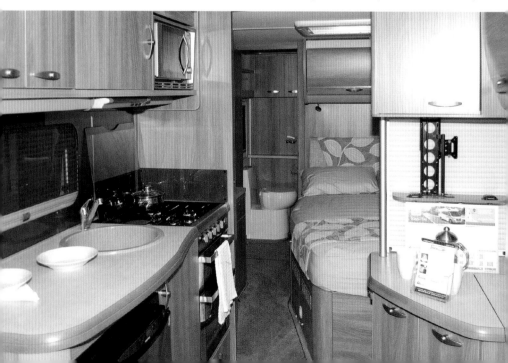

it's possible to separate the bedroom from the main body of the van, providing some privacy. After a long hike you can fall into bed without the need to play 'let's rearrange the furniture.'

There are three positions for a fixed bed:

1) Across the rear of the motorhome, above what could be considered a garage, if one is fitted. The height of the 'garage' determines how many steps are needed to climb into bed. In this case, access could be rather difficult if mobility is an issue.

2) Along one side of the motorhome, usually with the toilet/shower room next to it. This isn't favoured by some because the corner of the bed has usually been done away with to allow better access to the toilet. Also, there's a lack of privacy when the toilet is in use.

3) An island bed with access to both sides and with the headboard at the rear of the motorhome. This type of fixed bed tends to be found in much larger motorhomes, as room for the toilet compartment has to be found from elsewhere.

Fixed beds take up a fair amount of space, and therefore usually dictate a larger motorhome overall, when compared to a motorhome without a fixed bed but with the same amount of berths – ie: expect a four-berth with a fixed bed to be larger than a four-berth without.

If the fixed bed is in a medium-sized motorhome it generally replaces the U-shaped lounge at the rear, in which case the only other seating area is around the dinette, which may not prove very comfortable if wet weather keeps you inside the motorhome all day.

End or middle bathroom?
End bathroom
The benefits of an end bathroom are that the motorhome doesn't give

Fig 7. Fixed bed (bathroom to side).

Fig 8. End bathroom.

toilet and shower to be used at the same time. Of course, there's nothing quite like being able to sit down and have a shower after a long and tiring day out. On the subject of showers, some modern vans have an external shower point, which can be handy for sluicing down children and dogs just back from the beach, or covered in mud.

The downside to end bathrooms is that it will most likely be close to the exterior door, so privacy could be a problem. Another consideration is does its location allow easy access, or would you need you to climb over others in the middle of the night to use the toilet? Also, if it's an older type of panel van conversion, it's possible, due to the way the cubicle door operates, that this may encroach into the living space.

Middle bathroom

The benefits of a middle bathroom are that you can have a dinette at the front which converts to a double bed, and a lounge at the rear that also makes a double bed. Occupants of both can use the bathroom at night without disturbing the other. One area may also have more privacy at night, as there may be a dividing door which separates the front dinette from the rear lounge. Some would say that this is ideal when there are small children on board, as you can put them to bed and close the door. Be aware, though, that if you have a double

the impression of being split in two, with (probably) a dinette at the front and a U-shaped lounge at the back, separated by the bathroom on one side and the wardrobe on the other. Everybody can sit, talk, and eat together, no matter what the seating arrangements. If the bathroom is the width of the motorhome, there's the possibility of a separate toilet and shower cubicle, which would allow the

Fig 9. Middle bathroom.

Fig 10. Middle bathroom.

bed in the Luton top (the big hump over the driver's cab on a coachbuilt motorhome), and a dinette directly below and in front of it, you could find that the children fall onto each other while you're sound asleep in the rear.

Types of toilet
Whilst considering bathrooms, bear in mind that there are generally three different types of toilet:

Porta-potti
A fully portable toilet unit that consists of

Fig 11. Complete porta-potti ...

Fig 12. ... here split for emptying.

Fig 13. Bench toilet (normally cassette).

two parts, the top part contains the seat and a tank for holding flushing water, and the bottom a waste tank that can be removed for emptying.

Cassette toilet
This toilet is built into the motorhome, with an external access panel that allows the cassette waste tank to be removed for emptying. Water for flushing is taken from the clean water tank.

In more modern motorhomes, the cassette toilet may have an SOG ventilation unit

Fig 14. Swivel toilet (cassette).

Fig 15. Cassette access.

Fig 16. Cassette removal for emptying.

fitted which vents odours from the toilet to the outside. The decomposition process for the waste tank contents is accelerated by the increased flow of oxygen, thereby doing away with the need for chemicals. Be aware, however, that the SOG unit may ventilate into your awning, or in the direction of the neighbouring motorhome, depending on where the outlet is.

Note, also, that some types of cassette, for both porta-potti and cassette toilets, can be very awkward and heavy to carry when full, so bear in mind where the emptying point is when choosing your pitch. Alternatively, you could always empty the cassette on a daily basis.

SOG units are available in kit form for DIY installation, should you wish to add one to your existing motorhome.

Marine toilet

Like a cassette toilet, this is built into the motorhome. A large waste tank fitted to the underside of the van is normally emptied via a large-bore waste pipe that connects to the bottom of the tank, and then fed into an RV waste point. Obviously, the site you're intending to use must have such a point in order to

Fig 17. Swivel toilet (marine).

Fig 18. Waste pipe stored in sealed holder.

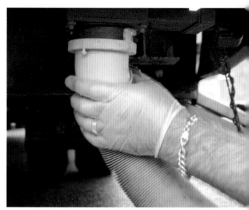

Fig 19. Waste pipe attached, ready to open valve to drain.

facilitate emptying of the unit, otherwise you could be carrying a lot of extra weight.

End or middle kitchen?
End kitchen
Essentially, the same benefits as with an end bathroom, the downside being

that this usually means the kitchen is right next to the door, which may be a problem if folk are coming in and out whilst the kitchen is being used. This location does allow good ventilation, of course, and the van won't fill with

Fig 20. End kitchen.

Fig 21. End kitchen.

cooking smells. Some motorhomes have the kitchen at the rear but on the opposite side to the door, which makes entry and exit much easier whilst the kitchen is in use.

Middle kitchen

Benefits include: no problem with entry/exit; the kitchen area may be slightly larger than with an end kitchen, because it tends to sit between the front passenger seat and the exterior door (an end kitchen is more likely to sit between the side wall and the toilet/shower cubicle, across the width of the motorhome).

An added benefit it that the chef is not normally stood with his or her back to the rest of the van, so can take part in any conversation; being close to the door, it's easier to see what's happening outside,

Fig 22. Middle kitchen.

Fig 23. Middle kitchen.

Fig 25. Four-burner and oven.

Fig 24. Three-burner, no grill.

which is especially helpful if you have an awning where the children are playing.

On the subject of kitchens, note that the cooking equipment supplied varies considerably. Small van conversions and most imported motorhomes generally have only two or three gas rings, eiother with or without a grill. It would appear that European motorhomers either eat out or have a BBQ (most will have an external gas point). Would this be enough for you, or do you want the whole cooking experience of four rings (maybe three gas and one electric), grill, and full size oven with an overhead extractor fan?

In the space where one motorhome has an oven, another may have a cupboard instead,

Fig 26. Four-burner grill and oven.

unless, of course, it's the full cooker option that tends to be fitted during van construction, with cupboards, etc, arranged around it. If no oven is supplied and you would like one, a gas oven can normally be easily fitted after purchase.

Another consideration is seating: should you opt for the standard dinette or bench-style seating with a free-standing table? A standard dinette, with the table between the seats, may seem at first to be a good set-up, great for the children because you can pin them in the corners to prevent them running around when they should be eating, but can

you relax in the evening in this upright position? With the bench seats and free-standing table arrangement, the table can be removed easily to allow you to stretch out on the benches and relax (if you can control the children, that is!).

Other considerations

Water tanks
Clean water: fed to the sinks, built-in toilets and shower
If you have this you will require some means of filling it; the majority of people tend to use a new garden hose,

although you can purchase special, blue, food quality hose if you wish, although the majority of motorhomers don't tend to drink the water from their clean water tanks.

Grey water: waste water from the sinks and shower

On-board tank usually emptied using a supplied hose (normally a 6 foot length of 4 inch diameter concertina pipe). If the tank is not on board then the external tank will be coloured black and hold about five gallons. Probably best to empty this on a daily basis due to its weight when full! It is illegal to empty grey water on the public highway.

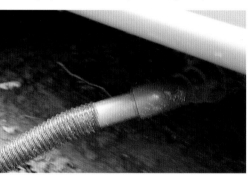

Fig 27. Emptying grey water.

Black water: waste water from the toilet

If this is in a cassette then there's no problem with emptying it at the site chemical disposal point (CDP). If you have a marine toilet, this is emptied in the same way as the on-board grey water tank using a similar type of pipe, but emptied into an RV dump point.

It is illegal to empty black water on the public highway: if the site doesn't have an RV toilet dump, ask if you can empty the cassette via a sewer outlet.

If all or some of these are not already on-board, ensure you have all the relevant tanks, connectors and pipes. Whilst undoubtedly convenient to have all of these tanks on-board, bear in mind their weight when full; most motorhomers fill up with fresh water on arrival at their site and empty all water tanks before departing.

Types of gas for cooking and heating

There are three types of 'gas' available in the UK: autogas, butane and propane.

Autogas is used via either an inbuilt LPG gas tank or in a refillable cylinder – normally yellow in colour – the sizes of which are 6kg or 11kg. Butane is

Fig 28. 13kg propane cylinder in locker.

available in sizes of 4.5kg, 7kg, 12kg and 15kg in a blue cylinder, and propane in an orange cylinder in sizes of 3.9kg, 6kg,13kg, 19kg and 47kg.

Propane (orange cylinder) freezes at a lower temperature than does butane, so is therefore the preferred gas for all-year touring; the 13kg cylinder is the most commonly-used size. Note that the weight stated on the front of the cylinder is the weight of the gas, and does not include the weight of the cylinder. To determine how much gas you have in a cylinder, look at the tally disc on the handle, as this will tell you the weight of the cylinder when empty. Weigh the cylinder you have and deduct this figure from the total weight to give you the amount of gas in the cylinder. Most motorhomes have the facility to carry one or two cylinders in an outside locker.

Ensure you have the correct regulator for the type of gas you intend to use (these are also colour-coded). Gas cylinders are extremely heavy, which could well decide whether you really want or need to carry two cylinders.

To give an indication of how long the gas will last, a 15kg cylinder will provide 3kW of continuous heat for approximately 68 hours.

Make sure you get a current safety certificate for the gas installation.

Electrics
Mains electric
If the vehicle is fitted with a mains unit, are you happy that it's properly installed? Is there a lead for connecting to site electrics (usually coloured orange)? You might be surprised at the number of previous owners who take these for their next

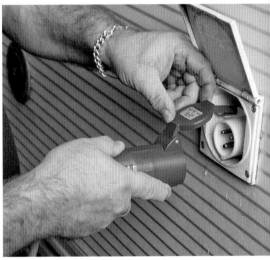

Top: Fig 29. Mains supply cable.

Above: Fig 30. Motorhome connection.

Right: Fig 31. Site connection.

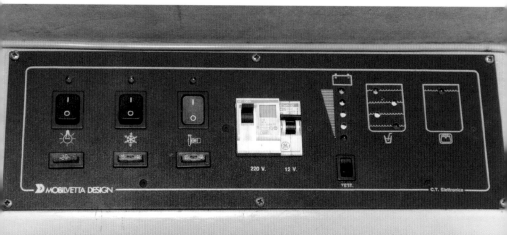

Fig 32. Basic fuse panel and battery condition indicator.

motorhome. Does the mains unit have a facility to charge the leisure battery/batteries, and/or the vehicle battery? Remember that the site supply will normally be 16 amps, which is a lot lower than that in a house. So if you have on the microwave, television and satellite box, fridge and the hot water, don't be surprised if you trip out the site supply!

If a mains lead is present it should look similar to that shown in Fig 29; whilst you can purchase the parts to make your own lead, the site owner would expect to see something that looked like this; ie blue plugs and sockets and orange, high visibility, weatherproof cable. Not all cable is the same, and he's perfectly within his rights to ask you to remove it if it does not appear correct.

If mains electricity is present in the motorhome be sure to get a current safety certificate. There's nothing worse than buying a motorhome, and have your insurance insist on a habitation check, only to find that the installation isn't correct.

Leisure battery/batteries
Are there any batteries? If so, are they securely fitted and in good order? Ask the seller how these are charged: by a mains unit, split charger from the alternator when driving, or via a solar panel? Leisure batteries tend to be larger, ie in the region of 105 amp hours and higher. If there's more than one it's recommended they be the same make, age and size in amp hours to give more chance of them being balanced, and receiving equal amounts when charging. One thing to note is that a leisure battery is not the same as a car battery: the car battery is designed to provide a large amount of power for a short period of time, and a leisure battery is designed to provide power over a longer period of time. It used to be said that a good leisure battery will weigh considerably more than a car battery, because, due to its intended extended power output, it will have considerably thicker plates. That said, if you're a weekend motorhomer, you may find that a car battery can meet all your power needs.

Inverters

These are small electrical units that convert 12 volts to 240 volts. They come in a variety of sizes from 100 watts to 2000 watts. Whilst handy for the odd use of a mains item, they're not recommended for continual usage, as with a small electric heater or a television that's on all day. Most have a low battery warning that sounds if the voltage drops to 10.5 volts.

If you intend to purchase one of these, or there is an inverter in the motorhome, be aware that there are two types: modified sine wave and pure sine wave. Those that produce a 'pure' sine wave output are recommended for items such as computers and televisions. Bear in mind that if, for instance, you want to run a microwave oven, although it may be rated at 800 watts, on start-up it could draw up to 50 per cent more current: that's 1200-1300 watts in total, so consider carefully what size inverter to buy. Although small inverters up to 200 watts can be plugged into your 12-volt socket, larger ones should be permanently fitted as close as possible to the battery.

Solar panel/s

If one or more of these are fitted, there will be a controller/regulator panel that will show output in both volts and amps, and if they are charging the batteries. If these are the really small panels, they are intended to provide a trickle charge to maintain a battery, as opposed to bringing the battery to full voltage. Solar panels – dependent on their size – can be wired to charge both drive and leisure batteries, as well as provide current to the motorhome's 12-volt electrical system.

Fig 33. Solar panel controller.

The consensus of opinion is that, if not already fitted, solar panels are a worthwhile addition, and they are available as DIY kits in a vast array of sizes and prices. If you intend fitting your own, keep in mind the weight of the units you buy, as this will affect your overall payload.

Fuel cells

The most common unit on the market at the moment is the Efoy fuel cell generator, which generates power to charge your leisure batteries automatically, as and when the voltage drops below a set level. The Efoy unit requires a fuel cell with 5 litres of methanol to provide the power: one fuel cell will provide a 40 watt unit with continuous power for approximately 7 to 8 days, at a cost of approximately £22-£26 at today's rates, giving an output of 130 amp hours a day, sufficient to charge a leisure battery or batteries up to a total of 160 amp hours in size (all power ratings are based on the Efoy comfort 80). Virtually silent in operation, the cost of the fuel cell is comparable to that of a week's mains hook-up. The generation process is totally pollutant- and emissions-free.

Downside is that the cost of the main unit is around £2000-£2500, plus installation costs for an Efoy comfort 80, although it is possible to DIY-install. Additionally, at the time of writing it is not permitted to carry methanol through the channel tunnel in a motorhome, and some insurance companies will not insure you if you carry more than 5 litres on board, so be aware of this if a unit is fitted!

Generators

Generators can be either gas-, diesel- or petrol-driven. Gas is the quietest but also the most expensive, whilst some diesel and petrol generators can be extremely noisy, even when fitted with a silencer. As for value for money, none of them is really efficient at providing mains voltage, when compared to an electric hook-up. Consider also the weight of the generator and fuel, and how you might transport petrol or diesel.

Most commercial sites do not allow the use of generators, and, if they do, usage will be restricted to certain times.

If you are not intending to wild camp all year you may decide there's no real need for a generator.

Wind power

You can purchase wind generator kits for motorhomes, but, as with fuelled generators, these can constitute a large expense for little gain. A major problem is securing it to withstand the level of wind speed it requires to operate at a satisfactory level, and also precisely *where*

you can site it, especially in relation to your neighbours: in the wrong position the vanes can produce an excessive amount of noise.

Charging leisure batteries

A dual charger will charge both vehicle and leisure batteries from the mains at the same time. A split charger will charge the vehicle battery first, and then pass any excess charge to the leisure batteries from the alternator.

As already stated, solar panels can be wired to trickle charge either the leisure batteries and/or the vehicle battery.

Fridges and freezers

Do you need a fridge? If only short trips are planned, a 12-volt-operated cool box running from your car cigarette lighter socket may suffice, if you don't already have a fitted fridge.

Most modern fridges/freezers can be run by gas, 12 volts or mains electric, but be aware the 12-volt setting is only for use when the vehicle is in motion, and will only maintain the existing temperature of the fridge. For this reason, prior to leaving always chill your food and, if possible, run the fridge

Fig 34. Fridge control for gas: A = Gas on/off; B = Fridge temp; C = Gas ignition.

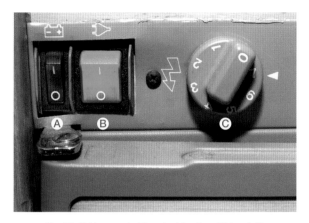

Fig 35. Fridge control for electric: A = 12V on/off;
B = Mains on/off; C = Fridge temp when on electric.

cooling too much and forcing the heat exchanger to work overtime. They also prevent the usual bugs and insects from taking up residence in the gas burner!

Heating
If it is your intention to travel all year round, then heating could be a major consideration.

Types of heating
If you intend to always stay on a site which has

on mains electricity or gas for a couple of hours to cool it.

If you decide that a fridge is needed, they are available in a variety guises, although size is generally dictated by overall size of the motorhome. For example, a small panel van or small coachbuilt vehicle may have just a small fridge; a bigger coachbuilt or small A-Class van could have a fridge with a small, built-in freezer section. A large coachbuilt A-Class or RV could have a full-size fridge and a full-size freezer. If your intended motorhome has a fridge fitted, check that the cold weather screens are there; these are used to cover the vents when the outside temperature drops below 50 degrees F and when the motorhome is in storage, and help prevent the fridge

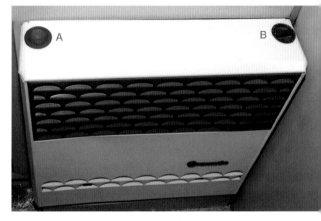

Fig 36. Basic convector: A = Blanking plate;
B = Gas ignition and temp control.

Fig 37. Blower controls for hot air:
A = Continuous; B = Blower off;
C = Blower controlled by thermostat.

Fig 38. Dual fuel convector: A = Gas ignition and temp control; B = Blower control for hot air.

a mains electric hook-up, a small, portable, electric fan heater will provide almost instant heat.

Probably the most popular form of heating is gas, in the shape of a small convector heater in a older motorhome, or a convector heater with a blown air system to provide heating

Fig 39. Dual controls for heating and hot water (heater control arrowed): thermostat (inner ring) and 1kW, 2kW or 3kW mains (outer ring).

throughout the van in a more modern one. Whilst this provides a good source of heating, it is a dry heat, and the electricity needed to power the fan or fans can place a heavy load on your leisure batteries. Also, if the temperature sensor is not correctly sited, it may turn off the power before the whole van is warm. Some blown air systems can seem noisy, but this is a subjective view, as is whether or not they are good at blowing dust around the interior!

Something that has been around for a couple of years, and which is being fitted again in new vans is a 'wet heating system,' which comprises a boiler and a system of 'radiators' placed throughout the van. The boiler can be gas and/or mains electric, and a pump circulates hot water through the radiators. Users say that this arrangement is as good as, if not better, than the blown air system, because the heat is better and more evenly distributed around the van, and the system is quieter.

The only downside is that the system takes longer to warm the van because the radiator pipes run around the base of the walls, and in the back of lockers, etc, but once the van is warm it maintains a better temperature because the hot water is continually circulating.

Whilst on the subject of heating and keeping warm, most modern and some older imported models have silver window blinds fitted to provide better insulation on the habitation windows, though few have anything for the windscreen.

You can purchase 'silver screens' for these – and there are many different makes and styles – but it all comes down to whether you want internal- or

Fig 40. Window silver screen.

Top: Fig 41. External silver screen.

Above: Fig 42. Internal silver screen.

Fig 43. Internal screen suction cup.

GPS holders – will, of course, prevent the screen from fitting correctly. Internal screens are usually held in place by suckers.

As with external fitting screens (which are made of a much stronger and heavier material to withstand all weathers) can you store them if it has been pouring with rain all night, and they are soaking wet? External screens are attached by a corner flap that fits over the top of the door, and a loop around the wing mirror and behind the wiper blades. If external screens are left in place all the winter, they do tend to provide a home for every type of insect you can think of!

Both types of screen have the added advantage of not only insulating the area, but also acting as blackout blinds. If you find the cost of silver screens prohibitive, there are websites

external-fitting screens. If external-fitting screens are what's required, it's better to have them custom-made so that you get the best fit possible. Internal silver screens are lighter and take up less storage space when not in use. A small amount of condensation on the inside of the screen will still be present, and any fittings you may have on the inside of the windscreen – such as fans and

that show you how to make your own; some of the comments left by people who have done so suggest that this is neither too difficult nor expensive.

Hot water systems

These can be run by mains electric, 12 volt or gas, depending on make and type of water heater installed, to provide hot water for sink(s), showers, and, in some cases, central heating. One thing to bear in mind is the capacity of the hot water heating tank, as this can be as little as seven litres in older vans, meaning that you'll use water faster than it can heat it. If you like a long shower, try to use less hot water by not having the spray on full, turning the spray off when washing hair and body, and turning on again to rinse. Not only will this conserve some of your hot water, it will also use less water from your tank, which, if you are wild camping, you need every drop of! If your van has 240V hot water, the power switch for this will be situated near the actual water heater.

Note: Some gas-only Truma heaters and water heaters can be converted to run on mains electricity as well as gas. A conversion kit is available that can be fitted by any competent DIY-er.

Remember: Your comfort can make a vast difference to the success and enjoyment of your holiday, but decide for yourself what level this needs to be. I know of intrepid travellers who have spent five or six months travelling Europe in a Volkswagen weekender, so if it suits you, go for it!

Fig 44. Gas-only heater control; single-fuel boiler (switch in neutral position, as above = off).

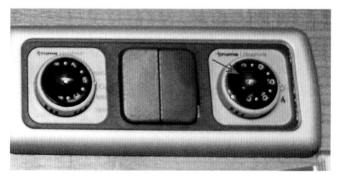

Fig 45. Dual controls for heating and hot water (hot water control arrowed): thermostat (inner ring) and 12V or gas (outer ring).

three
Small to medium size motorhomes

De-mountable
Not many of these about now, but can be handy if your usual mode of transport is a pick-up truck. These free-standing units are lowered onto the back of a pick-up truck: a few bolts and tensioners are secured, and away you go! A fully enclosed coachbuilt construction means there's no way of getting from the cab into the back without going outside. Usually two-berth, facilities may be sparse, as with the SWB van style: just the basic two-burner stove for cooking; no toilet. The main advantage is that it's not necessary to carry the living quarters all the time, and the pick-up can still be used as it was intended.

Professional panel van conversions, sometimes called B-Class
Short-wheelbase van: Volkswagen, Ford transit, etc
The older type of van conversions generally have only the absolute basics:

possibly a small sink or bowl, with a two-ring gas cooker and maybe a grill; a bench seat that converts into a double bed, and some storage. Clean and dirty water is held in external tanks. No full height standing room. Not usually affected by damp due to the fact they are built within the van's metal body. If you want just the basics – and maybe only weekends away – then these are worth considering. On the plus side they are not much bigger than a car and probably cost no more to run; great if you want it for everyday use.

Pop-top
As above but with a roof that can be raised when parked to give full standing height. Some have the potential for two small bunks in the raised roof space, so would be listed as a 2+2-berth (two adults and two children).
Some modern pop-tops (10 years old or less) come with two burner rings, grill and small oven, and a cassette

Motorhomes come in all shapes and sizes. These diagrams show the most common bed layouts.

(Drawings not to scale)

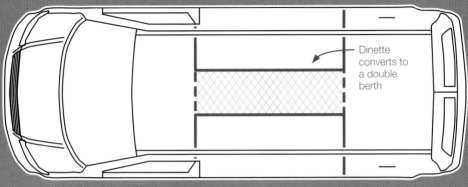

Dinette converts to a double berth

Fig Van1. Two-berth.

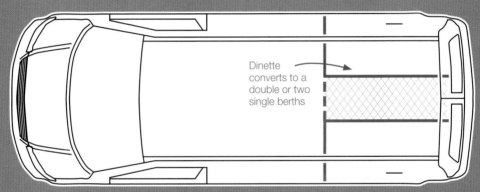

Dinette converts to a double or two single berths

Fig Van2. Two-berth.

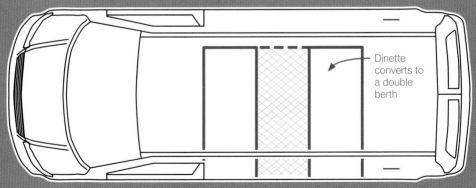

Dinette converts to a double berth

Fig Van3. Two-berth.

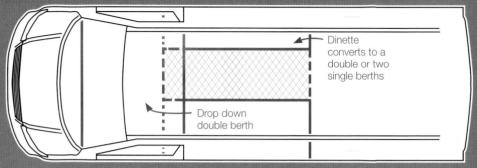

Dinette converts to a double or two single berths

Drop down double berth

Fig Van4. Four-berth A-Class.

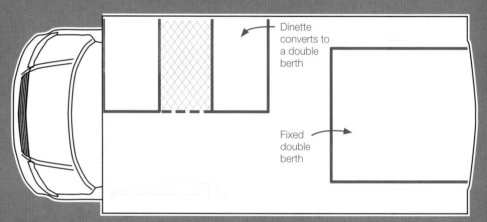

Dinette converts to a double berth

Fixed double berth

Fig Van5. Four-berth A- or C-Class.

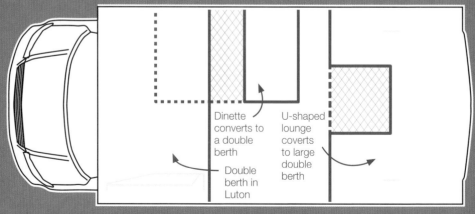

Dinette converts to a double berth

U-shaped lounge coverts to large double berth

Double berth in Luton

Fig Van6. Six-berth C-Class.

Fig 46. New-style pop-top circa 2010.

Left: Fig 47. Interior of new-style pop-top.

toilet or porta-potti, which gives more travel options.

High-top
Similar to the pop-top but with the added bonus of standing height in the rear at all times. and a full-size awning may be attached to the van if desired. If the full high-top area hasn't been converted to some form of sleeping

arrangement then storage space will probably be enhanced by fitted cupboards.

Long-wheelbase van: Ford, Renault, Iveco, etc
More room than in a SWB van due to increased length and because the majority are based on high top vans. Classed as a four-berth or luxury two-berth due to the room, and the facilities that can be fitted into the greater floor

Fig 48. Old-style pop-top circa 1980.

Fig 49. Older style high-top circa 1980.

Fig 50. Newer style high-top circa 2008.

Cold water only

Two-burner; no oven or grill

Fig 51. Interior new-style high-top.

Double berth

Fridge, no toilet

Fig 52. Interior new-style high-top.

Fig 53. Notice how space is increased by using swivel front seats as general seating.

area. Some even include a shower: no mean feat in a comparatively small space.

Damp is not a problem because the interior is built within the van's metal bodyshell, but, compared to a motorhome, it may appear narrow because the van was probably originally built for an entirely different role.

This type can be easier to park than larger motorhomes as it is no wider than a standard van, so will fit within a car park space widthways, although there may be an overhang in length.

DIY van conversion

This is definitely one for the DIY-er, as it's possible to buy the van of choice and build the interior to your specification. Sound good? There are drawbacks: you will need somewhere dry to store the van whilst you are building the interior; gas and/or electrical installations must be checked and certified safe by a qualified person;

insurance can also be a problem as not many companies are prepared to insure self-built vans; you could spend a fortune putting in all the items you require only to find you now have a van that exceeds its designated weight limit. It is possible to have the van re-plated, but companies that can do this are few and far between, and it does not come cheap. It could mean uprating both the axles and suspension, and your engine may not like it, either.

An alternative is to buy an interior in kit form for your chosen van; a number of companies supply these, and this route is still cheaper than purchasing a ready-converted motorhome. Insurance may be easier to obtain because the insurance companies are familiar with the kits and how they're made.

A quick search on the internet for 'DIY motorhomes' will provide all information you need, and also suppliers for the parts, etc.

Fig 54. Long-wheelbase (LWB).

Fig 55. Long-wheelbase interior.

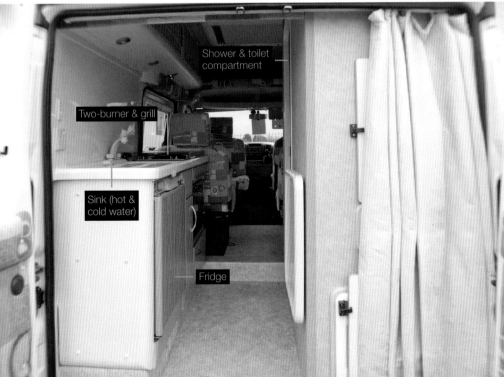

four

Medium to large size motorhomes

Coachbuilt also know as C-Class
'Coachbuilt' means that the body is built around a standard chassis and cab assembly. The vans tend to be quite large because they are more often than not based on a LWB chassis; some also

Fig 56. Coachbuilt 2010 (low profile two-berth).

Fig 57.
Coachbuilt
1990
(five-
berth).

Fig 58.
Coachbuilt
2000
(two-
berth).

47

Fig 59. Coachbuilt (four-berth).

have a tag-axle (double axle) at the rear. They are wider than a van conversion so extra care needs to be taken when – as is sometimes the case – the body can be up to 12-18 inches (30-40cm) wider than the cab itself (those that aren't wider than the cab are normally known as slim-line). Bodies tend to have an aluminium outer and a foam inner, with a finishing panel on the inside. If buying secondhand, check very carefully for damp, as it's not unknown for bodywork seams to leak. Small leaks can be remedied, but what appears to be a small leak on the inside can be a major leak inside the bodyshell.

It's possible to park without too much trouble (but be aware of where the overhang goes), although some newer car parks seem to have smaller spaces, so may not accommodate the extra width, let alone the length.

Modern coachbuilt motorhomes tend to have all that might be needed in the way of facilities: cassette toilet; shower; hot and cold running water; blown-air heating; leisure batteries, etc. If any of these are not fitted as standard, they can be added when and if required.

What do I mean by modern? Well, imported vans over 20 years old will have had all of the above facilities fitted during manufacture, but the British were slow to emulate this, so, in this instance, modern means 10-15 years old, and up to 28 feet (8.53 metres) in length.

Low profile C-Class
Has all the fittings of a full-size coachbuilt but with a lower roof (though full standing height still). The Luton box over the cab is missing, though there may well be a degree of storage area. Normally classed as

Above: Fig 60. New low profile circa 2011 (two-berth).   Below: Fig 61. Low profile interior.

High level storage

Two single or double berth

Above: Fig 62. Low profile interior circa 2000 (two-berth, end kitchen).

Below: Fig 63. Low profile interior (four-berth, middle kitchen).

a luxury two-berth or four-berth. If the vehicle is based on a larger van chassis there could be a fixed double bed toward the rear. The reduced height may make the van lighter and more aerodynamic, and therefore able to return improved mpg.

Just on the market at the time of writing is a new type of low profile motorhome with a pop-top on the roof that provides more berths without increasing the overall size. Perhaps the downside of this can be seen in the accompanying photo Fig 65, showing the access route! The steps seem decidedly steep, so perhaps the berths are not for the faint-hearted, though I expect children would love them!

Fig 64. Low profile with pop-top.

Full size C-Class

Based on a cab and chassis assembly that has a Luton box on top of the cab, which allows a four-berth to become a six-berth by having the Luton fitted out as a double bed. On some of the four-berth models the Luton is used for storage. Obviously, these are larger types of van, so things like fuel, storage, parking and insurance will probably cost more than for a smaller van.

This type of motorhome comes in a multitude of configurations – luxury two-berth, four-berth, six-berth, fixed bed, etc – all available in many different layouts. Some have what is classed as

Left:
Fig 66.
Coachbuilt
with Luton
box.

Below:
Fig 67.
Interior
looking
towards
rear ...

Microwave

Full cooker

Two single or
double berth

Sink

Double berth

Shower & toilet

a 'garage' in the rear where almost anything can be stored and carried – even a motor scooter or motorcycle. The downside to having this garage is that the rear berths may be quite high, making them less accessible (note the angle of steps/ladder in Figs 70-72), although one or two motorhomes currently on the market have an hydraulic unit that allows the rear berths above the garage to be raised and lowered, making access easier if the garage is not in use or only partly filled.

Fig 68. ... and interior looking towards front.

Fig 69. A standard dinette/two-berth unit (see Fig Van5 on page 38) has been converted to a small L-shaped dinette to allow wheelchair access.

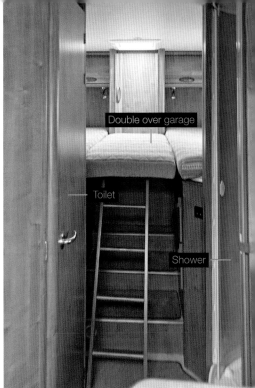

Above: Fig 70. Over-garage; double.

Below: Fig 72. Over-garage; double.

Above: Fig 71. Over-garage; steps for use as two singles, ladder for use as a double.

five

Large to extra-large size motorhomes

A-Class
Generally classed as the biggest type of motorhome manufactured in the UK and Europe, A-Class motorhomes are built from the chassis up: the driving position is built into the main body of the vehicle. This allows the room above the driving position to be optimised with

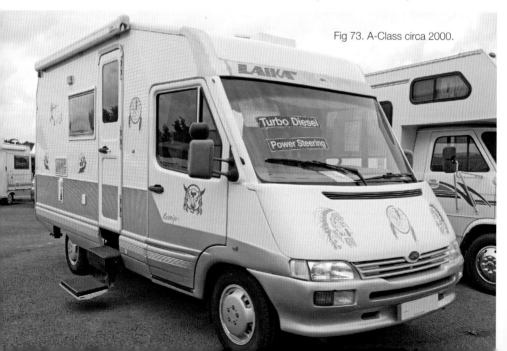

Fig 73. A-Class circa 2000.

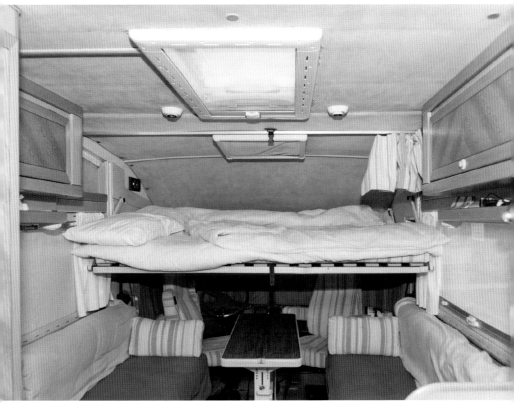

Fig 74. Over-cab bed down.

the addition of a dropdown double bed, thereby giving more room in the rear, and making the whole van deceptively large. Normally classed as a four- or even a six-berth; some may even have a fixed bed toward the rear as well.

The most commonly imported makes are Hymer and Pilote, although there are others, all of which tend to utilise the full legal width of over 7 feet allowed on UK roads, and between 18 and 28 feet in length. One of the main advantages of the A-Class is the dropdown bed, because if a quick departure is necessary, this can be left made up in the travelling position: additionally, should you arrive late at

your destination, you can lower it and jump straight in, with no shifting of tables, cushions, bedding to sort, etc.

A couple of things to note with regard to the A-Class is that some upper storage space is lost where the dropdown bed is stored, but this is offset by the greater amount of floor space that's made available with the bed out of the way. Check that you can access the dropdown double bed, as some can be deceptively high: is there a ladder, or might you end up not using the bed but making up the lower dinette bed instead?

Where will you store the motorhome? A-Class models are not

Fig 75. Five-berth layout.

Fig 76. Over cab bed up.

small so you may have to consider storage away from home, which can affect your insurance premium. Check if you do intend to store it on your drive that your house doesn't have a covenant that prohibits this.

Fifth wheel

There are some who wouldn't regard this as a motorhome because it is towed, but, given the standard to which it is built, it's worth consideration.

An interesting style which probably emanated from America, a large, powerful pick-up truck is a necessity with one of these. The motorhome unit is in the form of a trailer which pivots on an assembly welded into the rear pick-up bay of the truck: to all intents and purposes an articulated unit. The trailer unit is a modern, coachbuilt design: a single fibreglass assembly that can have slide-

Fig 77. A-Class circa 1990.

Fig 78. A-Class circa 1995.

Fig 79. Fifth wheel with open 'garage' at rear.

outs: side units that slide out at the push of a button to increase the interior floor area. They can be six- or eight-berth, with some having a fixed double bed over the pivot unit. As they are free-standing, the truck can be used as and when required, albeit with a large greasy pivot unit in the back.

Fig 80. Fifth wheel; front of unit.

Capable of providing all the comforts of home, you still need to consider where you will store it when not in use, as it throws up the same sort of problems as a large A-Class. Mpg has to be a consideration when going for something like this: those big pick-up trucks are gas-guzzlers.

American style RV
It might once have been said that if you can afford one of these then you don't need me to tell you about them. This doesn't appear to be the case any more, at least with a secondhand unit.

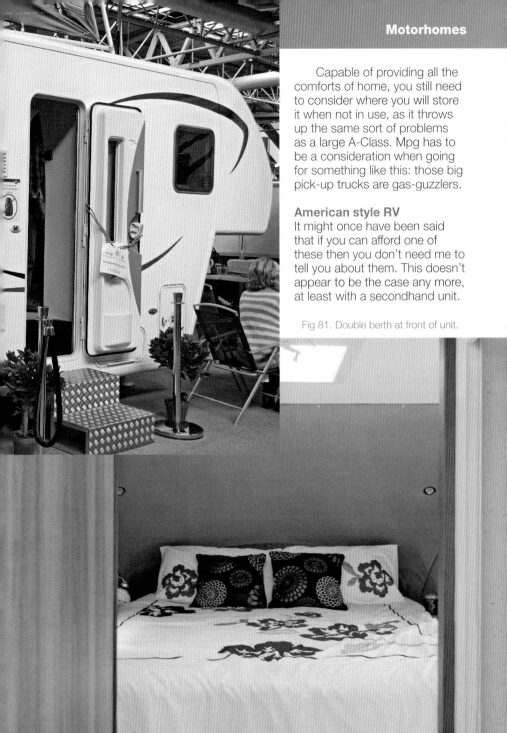

Fig 81. Double berth at front of unit.

Fig 82. Fifth wheel kitchen and lounge layout; note that the area to the right is contained in a slide out!

Fig 84. RV (standard body without slide outs).

Fig 83. RV with slide-outs.

Whilst a new unit can cost upward of £250,000, the price of a secondhand RV is comparable to that of a secondhand coachbuilt motorhome.

Usually fitted out with everything required to provide all the comforts of home (full-size bath, fridge, freezer, cooker, on board water tanks and generator), most of the newer models have one or two slide-outs in addition.

Points to consider: size (and whether this will limit where you can go); where you will store it; can you park when you get to your destination(s); fuel consumption.

It seems that many RV owners rent out their house, and use the income from this to tour Europe or further afield. When they have had enough they return home and sell the RV.

Fig 85. Standard RV lounge.

Fig 86. Standard RV kitchen.

Fig 87. Standard RV bedroom.

six
Extras & accessories

Awning

Quite what an awning should comprise is open to debate. Those who have owned caravans might reasonably expect a motorhome awning to be the 'extra room' that it is with a caravan, but this is not necessarily so. A motorhome awning can be no more than a sunshade that winds out from the side of the motorhome, and is supported by legs at the outside corners, though it is easy to use and put away when not required.

Drive-away awning

This, by contrast, *is* a room, the open wall of which abuts the vehicle's side,

Fig 88. Sunshade.

and is held in place by pegs and guy ropes, some of which go over the roof of the motorhome. This arrangement allows you to drive away once the ropes have been disengaged, leaving the awning in place. Usually, a panel can be zipped into the open side to enclose the area, meaning you can leave items such as chairs and tables at the site. It also shows that although your motorhome is not there, the pitch is occupied.

Standard awning

This is a lightweight awning that attaches via an aluminium channel, in much the same way as does a caravan awning, and is very useful if you intend to stay in one place for a length of time because it provides extra room without too much extra weight. The awning is threaded along an aluminium channel at the top of the motorhome side wall, usually on the sunshade fitting.

Care should be taken when choosing one of these awnings as the height of the motorhome will be an important factor. If there's no aluminium channel for the awning, then this can be purchased from most caravan or motorhome suppliers for DIY application. Depending on where you wish to fit the awning, the required aluminum channel is available in either U or J section; your supplier can help you decide which you need. Standard awnings are comparatively lightweight, so are not recommended for year-round use.

The downside, of course, is that this type of awning would have to be completely dismantled in order to drive the motorhome.

Safari room

If your motorhome has a sunshade, it is possible to convert this into what is

Fig 89. Lightweight awning.

known as a safari room by adding side and front walls that can be purchased from the sunshade manufacturer.

Similar to the standard awning, it provides a fully enclosed space outside the motorhome, but is made of a much heavier material that makes it more suitable for year-round usage.

If you intend to have a safari room, remember to take into account that this extra weight will affect your motorhome's payload.

Levelling ramps and spirit level
These items are essential, even if you intend to camp only on sites with a hard-standing for your van.

You may be surprised how being only slightly out of level can affect your motorhome: sinks and showers won't drain properly, and if the bed isn't level, you'll soon know it as you may well fall out, or find that your feet are higher than your head!

Ramps are readily available in two general types: one is a straightforward ramp that you drive up on until your van is at the required height; a block is then placed behind the wheel and the handbrake applied; the other has three or four steps, and the height is adjusted by moving from one step to another.

Fig 92. Dual electric steps.

Fig 90. Levelling ramp.

Fig 91. Single electric step.

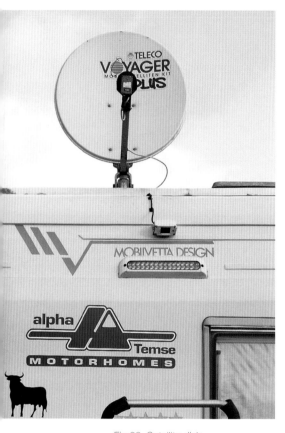

Fig 93. Satellite dish.

Fig 94. Internal satellite positioning control.

Pole rotates to face the dish in the correct direction

Crank to adjust dish angle (marked in deg)

If you have purchased a high-bodied motorhome then you may like to consider an electric step or steps. These can be really handy as long as you have some form of indicator on the dash that reminds you when they are extended!

Satellite dishes and television ariels

These can be either free-standing on a tripod, or permanently attached to the roof. If permanently attached, there's generally the facility to adjust height and angle from within the motorhome, similar to those shown in Fig 94.

Fig 95. Common television ariel.

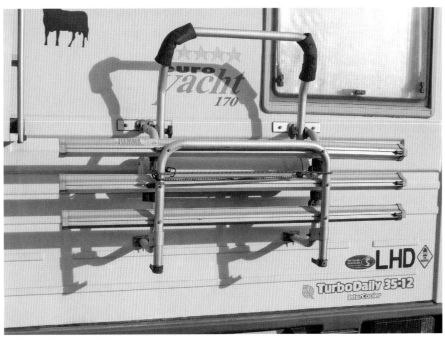

Fig 96. Cycle rack.

Cycle rack
If not already fitted, it's recommended that this is fitted by a professional, who should have a better understanding of the rear wall construction, and can ensure it is correctly supported.

Ladders and roof racks
Likewise, if not already fitted, it's recommended that this is done by a professional, who should have a better understanding of the rear wall construction which will

Fig 97. Ladder. Note the security plate to stop people climbing up.

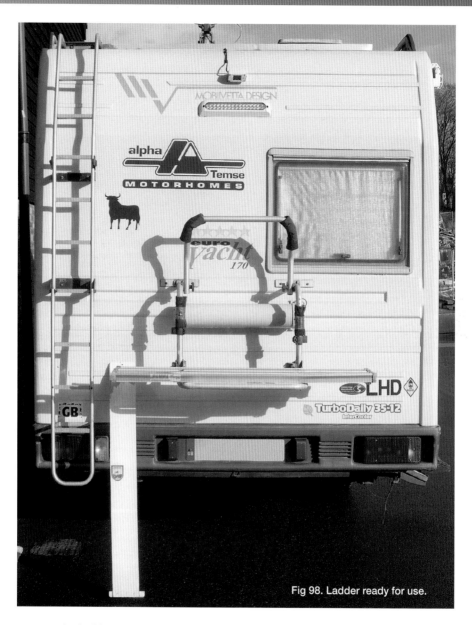

Fig 98. Ladder ready for use.

support the ladder, and can ensure the roof rack is correctly supported, as well as advise the maximum weight that can be carried on the roof (usually around 75kg).

Outside lockers
These are always a bonus, especially for storing things like boots, camping chairs, BBQ, etc. Some external lockers even allow access from inside the

Fig 99. External locker with internal access.

motorhome, so, If fitting an alarm system and your vehicle has these lockers, always ensure they are included within the alarm system.

Motorhome safety (for your protection)
• Carbon monoxide monitor (recommended)
• Smoke detector (recommended)

Fig 100. External locker.

- Supplementary security locks fitted to all doors (recommended [see Fig 101])
- Alarm system that allows all external doors to be alarmed, but still allows movement inside

Fig 101. Supplementary security lock.

Vehicle breakdown cover
It appears usual among breakdown services that, if your vehicle weighs more than 3.5 tons, a relay service or get-you-home service is not offered. What is interesting, though, is that if you join either the Caravan Club or the Caravan and Camping Club and take out their breakdown cover, which is provided by the very same companies, vehicle weight is irrelevant ...

Additional items
Some items can be retro-fitted if not present, most of which are within the capability of the average DIY-er. The internet is a good source of information about DIY alterations and additions.

Start with those items that will conserve your 12-volt power: a second leisure battery; LCD lighting; solar panel(s). Even if your intention is always to stay on a site and use the electric hook-up provided, consider what would happen if you break down. If you've taken the necessary steps you'll have lots of 12-volt power for the TV or radio whilst waiting to get going again, and possibly a battery to jump-start your vehicle battery if its flat!

Always remember that anything you add will have an impact on your payload.

seven
Checklist

This checklist is provided to help you decide which main features are important to you; which ones you would like to be present upon purchase, and those you would be happy to fit yourself.

Mains electric*
Leisure battery
Split charger (for engine)
Solar panels
Inverter
Alarm
LCD lighting
Oven
Extractor fan over cooker
Onboard clean water tank
Onboard grey water tank
Onboard black water tank
Hot water system*
Shower
Outside shower facility
Heater (gas)*
Heater (electric)*
Blown-air heating

Seat belts for rear passengers*
Fixed bed
Roof rack and ladder (check with vehicle manufacturer)
Tow bar
Awning
Awning light
Drive-away awning
Safari room
Reversing camera
Reversing sensors
Silver screens
Blinds
Curtains
Capacity for two gas bottles*
Bulk LPG tank*
Cassette toilet
Marine toilet
Outside lockers
BBQ gas outlet*
Air ride suspension*
Fridge (3-way: gas, 12-volt, 240-volt)*

*Must be checked and certified for insurance purposes.

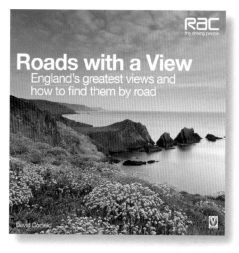
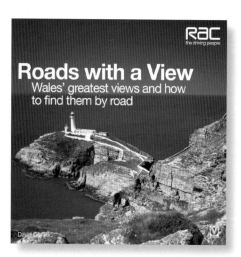

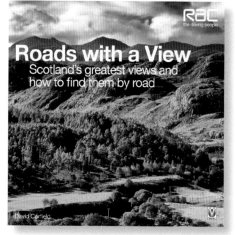

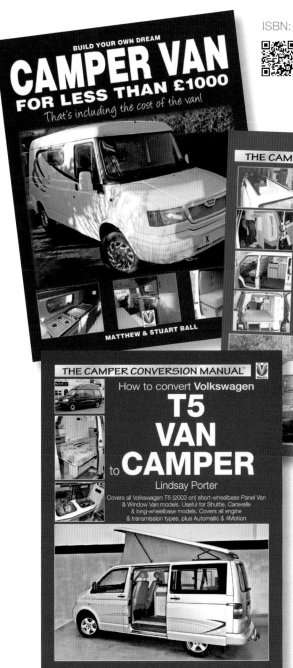

BUILD YOUR OWN DREAM

CAMPER VAN
FOR LESS THAN £1000
That's including the cost of the van!

MATTHEW & STUART BALL

ISBN: 978-1-845845-24-7

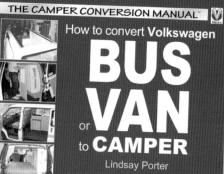

THE CAMPER CONVERSION MANUAL

How to convert **Volkswagen**

BUS
or VAN
to CAMPER

Lindsay Porter

Applies to all VW Transporter T3/T25 & T4 Panel Vans
& People Carriers (not Pick-up or Crew cab) 1980 to 2003

THE CAMPER CONVERSION MANUAL

How to convert **Volkswagen**

T5
VAN
to CAMPER

Lindsay Porter

Covers all Volkswagen T5 (2003 on) short-wheelbase Panel Van
& Window Van models. Useful for Shuttle, Caravelle
& long-wheelbase models. Covers all engine
& transmission types, plus Automatic & 4Motion

ISBN: 978-1-903706-45-9

ISBN: 978-1-904788-67-6

Index